Christopher Columbus
And The New World Of His Discovery
Volume 3

\

FILSON YOUNG
[ZHINGOORA BOOKS]

About Author

Alexander Bell Filson Young was a journalist, BBC programme advisor and author. His wrote the book on Titanic, a RMS Titanic ship. His famous works includeTitanic, The Relief of Mafekingand etc.

CHAPTER I

THE ENCHANTED ISLANDS

Columbus did not intend to remain long at San Salvador. His landfall there, although it signified the realisation of one part of his dream, was only the starting-point of his explorations in the New World. Now that he had made good his undertaking to "discover new lands," he had to make good his assurance that they were full of wealth and would swell the revenues of the King and Queen of Spain. A brief survey of this first island was all he could afford time for; and after the first exquisite impression of the white beach, and the blue curve of the bay sparkling in the sunshine, and the soft prismatic colours of the acanthus beneath the green wall of the woods had been savoured and enjoyed, he was anxious to push on to the rich lands of the Orient of which he believed this island to be only an outpost.

On the morning after his arrival the natives came crowding down to the beach and got down their canoes, which were dug out of the trunk of a single tree, and some of which were large enough to contain forty or forty-five men: They came paddling out to the ship, sometimes, in the case of the smaller canoes which only held one man, being upset by the surf, and swimming gaily round and righting their canoes again and bailing them out with gourds. They brought balls of spun cotton, and parrots and spears. All their possessions, indeed, were represented in the offerings they made to the strangers. Columbus, whose eye was now very steadily fixed on the main chance, tried to find out if they had any gold, for he noticed that some of them wore in their noses a ring that looked as though it were made of that metal; and by making signs he asked them if there was any more of it to be had. He understood them to say that to the south of the island there dwelt a king who had large vessels of gold, and a great many of them; he tried to suggest that some of the natives should come and show him the way, but he "saw that they were not interested in going."

The story of the Rheingold was to be enacted over again, and the whole of the evils that followed in its glittering train to be exemplified in this voyage of discovery. To the natives of these islands, who guarded the yellow metal and loved it merely for its shining beauty, it was harmless and powerless; they could not buy anything with it, nor did they seek by its aid to secure any other enjoyments but the happiness of looking at it and admiring it. As soon as the gold was ravished from their keeping, however, began the reign of lust and cruelty that always has attended and always will attend the knowledge that things can be bought with it. In all its history, since first it was brought up from the dark bowels of the earth to glitter in the light of day, there is no more significant scene than this that took place on the bright sands of San Salvador so long ago—Columbus attentively examining the ring in the nose of a happy savage, and trying to persuade him to show him the place that it was brought from; and the savage "not interested in going."

From his sign-conversation with the natives Columbus understood that there was land to the south or the south-west, and also to the north-west, and that the people from the north-west went to the south-west in search of gold and precious stones. In the meantime he determined to spend the Sunday in making a survey of the island, while the rest of Saturday was passed in barterings with the natives, who were very happy and curious to see all the strange things belonging to the voyagers; and so innocent were their ideas of value that "they give all they have for whatever thing may be given them." Columbus, however, who was busy making calculations, would not allow the members of the crew to take anything more on their own account, ordering that where any article of commerce existed in quantity it was to be acquired for the sovereigns and taken home to Spain.

Early on Sunday morning a boat was prepared from each ship, and a little expedition began to row north about the island. As they coasted the white rocky shores people came running to the beach and calling to them; "giving thanks to God," says Columbus, although this is probably a flight of fancy. When they saw that the boats were not coming to land they threw themselves into the water and came swimming out to them, bringing food and drink. Columbus noticed a tongue of land lying between the north-west arm of the internal lagoon and the sea, and saw that by cutting a canal through it entrance could be secured to a harbour that would float "as many ships as there are in Christendom." He did not, apparently, make a complete circuit of the island, but returned in the afternoon to the ships, having first collected seven natives to take with him, and got under way again; and before night had fallen San Salvador had disappeared below the north-west horizon.

About midday he reached another island to the southeast. He sailed along the coast until evening, when he saw yet another island in the distance to the south-west; and he therefore lay-to for the night. At dawn the next morning he landed on the island and took formal possession of it, naming it Santa Maria de la Concepcion, which is the Rum Cay of the modern charts. As the wind chopped round and he found himself on a lee-shore he did not stay there, but sailed again before night. Two of the unhappy prisoners from Guanahani at this point made good their escape by swimming to a large canoe which one of the natives of the new island had rowed out—a circumstance which worried Columbus not a little; since he feared it would give him a bad name with the natives. He tried to counteract it by loading with presents another native who came to barter balls of cotton, and sending him away again.

The effect of all that he was seeing, of the bridge of islands that seemed to be stretching towards the south-west and leading him to the region of untold wealth, was evidently very stimulating and exciting to Columbus. His Journal is almost incoherent where he attempts to set down all he has got to say. Let us listen to him for a moment:

"These islands are very green and fertile, and the breezes are very soft, and there may be many things which I do not know, because I did not wish to stop, in order to discover and search many islands to find gold. And since these people make signs thus, that they wear gold on their arms and legs,—and it is gold, because I showed them some pieces which I have,—I cannot fail, with the aid of our Lord, in finding it where it is native. And being in the middle of the gulf between these two islands, that is to say, the island of Santa Maria and this large one, which I named Fernandina, I found a man alone in a canoe who was going from the island of Santa Maria to Fernandina, and was carrying a little of his bread which might have been about as large as the fist, and a gourd of water, and a piece of reddish earth reduced to dust and afterwards kneaded, and some dry leaves—[Tobacco]—which must be a thing very much appreciated among them, because they had already brought me some of them as a present at San Salvador: and he was carrying a small basket of their kind, in which he had a string of small glass beads and two blancas, by which I knew that he came from the island of San Salvador, and had gone from there to Santa Maria and was going to Fernandina. He came to the ship: I caused him to enter it, as he asked to do so, and I had his canoe placed on the ship and had everything which he was carrying guarded and I ordered that bread and honey be given him to eat and something to drink. And I will go to Fernandina thus and will give him everything, which belongs to him, that he may give good reports of us. So that, when your Highnesses send here, our Lord pleasing, those who come may receive honour and the Indians will give them of everything which they have."

This hurried gabbling about gold and the aid of our Lord, interlarded with fragments of natural and geographical observation, sounds strangely across the gulf of time and impresses one with a disagreeable sense of bewildered greed—like that of a dog gulping at the delicacies in his platter and unwilling to do justice to one for fear the others should escape him; and yet it is a natural bewilderment, and one with which we must do our best to sympathise.

6

Fernandina was the name which Columbus had already given to Long Island when he sighted it from Santa Maria; and he reached it in the evening of Tuesday, October 16th. The man in the canoe had arrived before him; and the astute Admiral had the satisfaction of finding that once more his cleverness had been rewarded, and that the man in the canoe had given such glowing accounts of his generosity that there was no difficulty about his getting water and supplies. While the barrels of water were being filled he landed and strolled about in the pleasant groves, observing the islanders and their customs, and finding them on the whole a little more sophisticated than those of San Salvador. The women wore mantillas on their heads and "little pieces of cotton" round their loins-a sufficiently odd costume; and they appeared to Columbus to be a little more astute than the other islanders, for though they brought cotton in quantities to the ships they exacted payment of beads for it. In the charm and wonder of his walk in this enchanted land he was able for a moment to forget his hunger for gold and to admire the great branching palm-trees, and the fish that

"are here so different from ours that it is wonderful. There are some formed like cocks of the finest colours in the world, blue, yellow, red and of all colours, and others tinted in a thousand manners: and the colours are so fine, that there is not a man who does not wonder at them, and who does not take great pleasure in seeing them. Also, there are whales. I saw no beasts on land of any kind except parrots and lizards. A boy told me that he saw a large snake. I did not see sheep nor goats, nor any other beast; although I have been here a very short time, as it is midday, still if there had been any, I could not have missed seeing some."

Columbus was not a very good descriptive writer, and he has but two methods of comparison; either a thing is like Spain, or it is not like Spain. The verdure was "in such condition as it is in the month of May in Andalusia; and the trees were all as different from ours as day from night, and also the fruits and grasses and the stones and all the things." The essay written by a cockney child after a day at the seaside or in the country, is not greatly different from some of the verbatim passages of this journal; and there is a charm in that fact too, for it gives us a picture of Columbus, in spite of his hunt for gold and precious stones, wandering, still a child at heart, in the wonders of the enchanted world to which he had come.

There was trouble on this day, because some of the crew had found an Indian with a piece of gold in his nose, and they got a scolding from Columbus for not detaining him and bartering with him for it. There was bad weather also, with heavy rain and a threatening of tempest; there was a difference of opinion with Martin Alonso Pinzon about which way they should go round the island: but the next day the weather cleared, and the wind settled the direction of their course for them. Columbus, whose eye never missed anything of interest to the sailor and navigator, notes thus early a fact which appears in every book of sailing directions for the Bahama Islands—that the water is so clear and limpid that the bottom can be seen at a great depth; and that navigation is thus possible and even safe among the rockstrewn coasts of the islands, when thus performed by sight and with the sun behind the ship. He was also keenly alive to natural charm and beauty in the new lands that he was visiting, and there are unmistakable fragments of himself in the journal that speak eloquently of his first impressions. "The singing of the little birds is such that it appears a man would wish never to leave here, and the flocks of parrots obscure the sun."

But life, even to the discoverer of a New World, does not consist of wandering in the groves, and listening to the singing birds, and smelling the flowers, and remembering the May nights of Andalusia. There was gold to be found and the mainland of Cathay to be discovered, and a letter, written by the sovereigns at his earnest request, to be delivered to the Great Khan. The natives had told him of an island called Samoete to the southward, which was said to contain a quantity of gold. He sailed thither on the 19th, and called it Isabella; its modern name is Crooked Island. He anchored here and found it to be but another step in the ascending scale of his delight; it was greener and more beautiful than any of the islands he had yet seen. He spent some time looking for the gold, but could not find any; although he heard of the island of Cuba, which he took to be the veritable Cipango. He weighed anchor on October 24th and sailed south-west, encountering some bad weather on the way; but on Sunday the 28th he came up with the north coast of Cuba and entered the mouth of a river which is the modern Nuevitas. To the island of Cuba he gave the name of Juana in honour of the young prince to whom his son Diego had been appointed a page.

If the other islands had seemed beautiful to him, Cuba seemed like heaven itself. The mountains grandly rising in the interior, the noble rivers and long sweeping plains, the headlands melting into the clear water, and the gorgeous colours and flowers and birds and insects on land acted like a charm on Columbus and his sailors. As they entered the river they lowered a boat in order to go ahead and sound for an anchorage; and two native canoes put off from the shore, but, when they saw the boat approaching, fled again. The Admiral landed and found two empty houses containing nets and hooks and fishing-lines, and one of the strange silent dogs, such as they had encountered on the other island—dogs that pricked their ears and wagged their tails, but that never barked. The Admiral, in spite of his greed for gold and his anxiety to "free" the people of the island, was now acting much more discreetly, and with the genuine good sense which he always possessed and which was only sometimes obscured. He would not allow anything in the empty houses to be disturbed or taken away, and whenever he saw the natives he tried to show them that he intended to do them no harm, and to win their good will by making them presents of beads and toys for which he would take no return. As he went on up the river the scenery became more and more enchanting, so that he felt quite unhappy at not being able to express all the wonders and beauties that he saw. In the pure air and under the serene blue of the sky those matchless hues of blossom and foliage threw a rainbow-coloured garment on either bank of the river; the flamingoes, the parrots and woodpeckers and humming-birds calling to one another and flying among the tree-tops, made the upper air also seem alive and shot with all the colours of the rainbow. Humble Christopher, walking amid these gorgeous scenes, awed and solemnised by the strangeness and magnificence of nature around him, tries to identify something that he knows; and thinks, that amid all these strange chorusings of unknown birds, he hears the familiar note of a nightingale. Amid all his raptures, however, the main chance is not forgotten; everything that he sees he translates into some terms of practical utility. Just as on the voyage out every seaweed or fish or flying bird that he saw was hailed by him as a sign that land was near, so amid the beauty of this virgin world everything that he sees is taken to indicate either that he is close upon the track of the gold, or that he must be in Cipango, or that the natives will be easy to convert to Christianity. In the fragrance of the woods of Cuba, Columbus thought that he smelled Oriental spices, which Marco Polo had described as abounding in Cipango; when he walked by the shore and saw the shells of pearl oysters, he believed the island to be loaded with pearls and precious stones; when he saw a scrap of tinsel or bright metal adorning a native, he argued that there was a gold mine close at hand. And so he went on in an increasing whirl of bewildering enchantment from anchorage to anchorage and from island to island, always being led on by that yellow will o'-the-wisp, gold, and always believing that the wealth of the Orient would be his on the morrow. As he coasted along towards the west he entered the river which he called Rio de Mares. He found a large village here full of palm-branch houses furnished with chairs and hammocks and adorned with wooden masks and statues; but in spite of his gentleness and offer of gifts the inhabitants all fled to the mountains, while he and his men walked curiously through the deserted houses.

On Tuesday, October 30th, Martin Alonso Pinzon, whose communications the Admiral was by this time beginning to dread, came with some exciting news. It seemed that the Indians from San Salvador who were on board the Pinta had told him that beyond the promontory, named by Columbus the Cape of Palms, there was a river, four days' journey upon which would bring one to the city of Cuba, which was very rich and large and abounded with gold; and that the king of that country was at war with a monarch whom they called Cami, and whom Pinzon identified with the Great Khan. More than this, these natives assured him that the land they were on at present was the mainland itself, and that they could not be very far from Cathay. Columbus for once found himself in agreement with Martin Alonso. The well-thumbed copy of Marco Polo was doubtless brought out, and abundant evidence found in it; and it was decided to despatch a little embassy to this city in order to gain information about its position and wealth. When they continued their course, however, and rounded the cape, no river appeared; they sailed on, and yet promontory after promontory was opened ahead of them; and as the wind turned against them and the weather was very threatening they decided to turn back and anchor again in the Rio de Mares.

Columbus was now, as he thought, hot upon the track of the Great Khan himself; and on the first of November he sent boats ashore and told the sailors to get information from the houses; but the inhabitants fled shyly into the woods. Having once postulated the existence of the Great Khan in this immediate territory Columbus, as his habit was, found that everything fitted with the theory; and he actually took the flight of the natives, although it had occurred on a dozen other occasions, as a proof that they mistook his bands of men for marauding expeditions despatched by the great monarch himself. He therefore recalled them, and sent a boat ashore with an Indian interpreter who, standing in the boat at the edge of the water, called upon the natives to draw near, and harangued them. He assured them of the peaceable intentions of the great Admiral, and that he had nothing whatever to do with the Great Khan; which cannot very greatly have thrilled the Cubans, who knew no more about the Great Khan than they did about Columbus. The interpreter then swam ashore and was well received; so well, that in the evening some sixteen canoes came off to the ships bringing cotton yarn and spears for traffic. Columbus, with great astuteness, forbade any trading in cotton or indeed in anything at all except gold, hoping by this means to make the natives produce their treasures; and he would no doubt have been successful if the natives had possessed any gold, but as the poor wretches had nothing but the naked skins they stood up in, and the few spears and pots and rolls of cotton that they were offering, the Admiral's astuteness was for once thrown away. There was one man, however, with a silver ring in his nose, who was understood to say that the king lived four days' journey in the interior, and that messengers had been sent to him to tell him of the arrival of the strange ships; which messengers would doubtless soon return bringing merchants with them to trade with the ships. If this native was lying he showed great ingenuity in inventing the kind of story that his questioners wanted; but it is more likely that his utterances were interpreted by Columbus in the light of his own ardent beliefs. At any rate it was decided to send at once a couple of envoys to this great city, and not to wait for the arrival of the merchants. Two Spaniards, Rodrigo de Jerez and Luis de Torres, the interpreter to the expedition — who had so far found little use for his Hebrew and Chaldean—were chosen; and with them were sent two Indians, one from San Salvador and the other a local native who went as guide. Red caps and beads and hawks' bells were duly provided, and a message for the king was given to them telling him that Columbus was waiting with letters and presents from Spanish sovereigns, which he was to deliver personally. After the envoys had departed, Columbus, whose ships were anchored in a large basin of deep water with a clean and steep beach, decided to take the opportunity of having the vessels careened. Their hulls were covered with shell and weed; the caulking, which had been dishonestly done at Palos, had also to be attended to; so the ships were beached and hove down one at a time —an unnecessary precaution, as it turned out, for there was no sign of treachery on the part of the natives. While the men were making fires to heat their tar they noticed that the burning wood sent forth a heavy odour which was like mastic; and the Admiral, now always busy with optimistic calculations, reckoned that there was enough in that vicinity to furnish a thousand quintals every year. While the work on the ships was going forward he employed himself in his usual way, going ashore, examining the trees and vegetables and fruits, and holding such communication as he was able with the natives. He was up every morning at dawn, at one time directing the work of his men, at another going ashore after some birds that he had seen; and as dawn comes early in those islands his day was probably a long one, and it is likely that he was in bed soon after dark. On the day that he went shooting, Martin Alonso Pinzon was waiting for him on his return; this time not to make any difficulties or independent proposals, but to show him two pieces of cinnamon that one of his men had got from an Indian who was carrying a quantity of it. "Why did the man not get it all from him?" says greedy Columbus. "Because of the prohibition of the Admiral's that no one should do any trading," says Martin Alonso, and conceives himself to have scored; for truly these two men do not love one another. The boatswain of the Pinta, adds Martin Alonso, has found whole trees of it. "The Admiral then went there and found that it was not cinnamon." The Admiral was omnipotent; if he had said that it was manna they would have had to make it so, and as he chose to say that it was not cinnamon, we must take his word for it, as Martin Alonso certainly had to do; so that it was the Admiral who scored this time. Columbus, however, now on the track of spices, showed some cinnamon and pepper to the natives; and the obliging creatures "said by signs that there was a great deal of it towards the south-east." Columbus then showed them some gold and pearls; and "certain old men" replied that in a place they called Bo-No there was any amount of gold; the people wore it in their ears and on their arms and legs, and there were pearls also, and large ships and merchandise—all to the south-east. Finding this information, which was probably entirely untrue and merely a polite effort to do what was expected of them, well received, the natives added that "a long distance from there, there were men with one eye, and other men with dogs' snouts who ate men, and that when they caught a man they beheaded him and drank his blood" . . . Soon after this the Admiral went on board again and began to write up his Journal, solemnly entering all these facts in it. It is the most childish nonsense; but after all, how interesting and credible it must have been! To live thus smelling the most heavenly perfumes, breathing the most balmy air, viewing the most lovely scenes, and to be always hot upon the track of gold and pearls and spices and wealth and dog-nosed, blood-drinking monstrosities—what an adventure, what a vivid piece of living!

After a few days—on Tuesday, November 6th—the two men who had been sent inland to the great and rich city came back again with their report. Alas for visions of the Great Khan! The city turned out to be a village of fifty houses with twenty people in each house. The envoys had been received with great solemnity; and all the men "as well as the women" came to see them, and lodged them in a fine house. The chief people in the village came and kissed their hands and feet, hailing them as visitors from the skies, and seating them in two chairs, while they sat round on the floor. The native interpreter, doubtless according to instructions, then told them "how the Christians lived and how they were good people"; and I would give a great deal to have heard that brief address. Afterwards the men went out and the women came in, also kissing the hands and feet of the visitors, and "trying them to see if they were of flesh and of bone like themselves." The results were evidently so satisfactory that the strangers were implored to remain at least five days. The real business of the expedition was then broached. Had they any gold or pearls? Had they any cinnamon or spices? Answer, as usual: "No, but they thought there was a great deal of it to the south-east." The interest of the visitors then evaporated, and they set out for the coast again; but they found that at least five hundred men and women wanted to come with them, since they believed that they were returning to heaven. On their journey back the two Spaniards noticed many people smoking, as the Admiral himself had done a few days before; and this is the first known discovery of tobacco by Europeans.

They saw a great many geese, and the strange dogs that did not bark, and they saw potatoes also, although they did not know what they were. Columbus, having heard this report, and contemplating these gentle amiable creatures, so willing to give all they had in return for a scrap of rubbish, feels his heart lifted in a pious aspiration that they might know the benefits of the Christian religion. "I have to say, Most Serene Princes," he writes, "that by means of devout religious persons knowing their language well, all would soon become Christians: and thus I hope in our Lord that Your Highnesses will appoint such persons with great diligence in order to turn to the Church such great peoples, and that they will convert them, even as they have destroyed those who would not confess the Father and the Son and the Holy Spirit: and after their days, as we are all mortal, they will leave their realms—in a very tranquil condition and freed from heresy and wickedness, and will be well received before the Eternal Creator, Whom may it please to give them a long life and a great increase of larger realms and dominions, and the will and disposition to spread the holy Christian religion, as they have done up to the present time, Amen. To-day I will launch the ship and make haste to start on Thursday, in the name of God, to go to the southeast and seek gold and spices, and discover land."

Thus Christopher Columbus, in the Name of God,

November 11, 1492.

CHAPTER II

THE EARTHLY PARADISE

When Columbus weighed anchor on the 12th of November he took with him six captive Indians. It was his intention to go in search of the island of Babeque, which the Indians alleged lay about thirty leagues to the east-south-east, and where, they said, the people gathered gold out of the sand with candles at night, and afterwards made bars of it with a hammer. They told him this by signs; and we have only one more instance of the Admiral's facility in interpreting signs in favour of his own beliefs. It is only a few days later that in the same Journal he says, "The people of these lands do not understand me, nor do I nor any other person I have with me understand them; and these Indians I am taking with me, many times understand things contrary to what they are." It was a fault at any rate not exclusively possessed by the Indians, who were doubtless made the subject of many philological experiments on the part of the interpreter; all that they seemed to have learned at this time were certain religious gestures, such as making the Sign of the Cross, which they did continually, greatly to the edification of the crew.

In order to keep these six natives in a good temper Columbus kidnapped "seven women, large and small, and three children," in order, he alleged, that the men might conduct themselves better in Spain because of having their "wives" with them; although whether these assorted women were indeed the wives of the kidnapped natives must at the best be a doubtful matter. The three children, fortunately, had their father and mother with them; but that was only because the father, having seen his wife and children kidnapped, came and offered to go with them of his own accord. This taking of the women raises a question which must be in the mind of any one who studies this extraordinary voyage—the question of the treatment of native women by the Spaniards. Columbus is entirely silent on the subject; but taking into account the nature of the Spanish rabble that formed his company, and his own views as to the right which he had to possess the persons and goods of the native inhabitants, I am afraid that there can be very little doubt that in this matter there is a good reason, for his silence. So far as Columbus himself was concerned, it is probable that he was innocent enough; he was not a sensualist by nature, and he was far too much interested and absorbed in the principal objects of his expedition, and had too great a sense of his own personal dignity, to have indulged in excesses that would, thus sanctioned by him, have produced a very disastrous effect on the somewhat rickety discipline of his crew. He was too wise a master, however, to forbid anything that it was not in his power to prevent; and it is probable that he shut his eyes to much that, if he did not tolerate it, he at any rate regarded as a matter of no very great importance. His crew had by this time learned to know their commander well enough not to commit under his eyes offences for which he would have been sure to punish them.

For two days they ran along the coast with a fair wind; but on the 14th a head wind and heavy sea drove them into the shelter of a deep harbour called by Columbus Puerto del Principe, which is the modern Tanamo. The number of islands off this part of the coast of Cuba confirmed Columbus in his profound geographical error; he took them to be "those innumerable islands which in the maps of the world are placed at the end of the east." He erected a great wooden cross on an eminence here, as he always did when he took possession of a new place, and made some boat excursions among the islands in the harbour. On the 17th of November two of the six youths whom he had taken on board the week before swam ashore and escaped. When he started again on his voyage he was greatly inconvenienced by the wind, which veered about between the north and south of east, and was generally a foul wind for him. There is some difference of opinion as to what point of the wind the ships of Columbus's time would sail on; but there is no doubt that they were extremely unhandy in anything approaching a head wind, and that they were practically no good at all at beating to windward. The shape of their hulls, the ungainly erections ahead and astern, and their comparatively light hold on the water, would cause them to drift to leeward faster than they could work to windward. In this head wind, therefore, Columbus found that he was making very little headway, although he stood out for long distances to the northward. On Wednesday, November 21st, occurred a most disagreeable incident, which might easily have resulted in the Admiral's never reaching Spain alive. Some time in the afternoon he noticed the Pinta standing away ahead of him in a direction which was not the course which he was steering; and he signalled her to close up with him. No answer, however, was made to his signal, which he repeated, but to which he failed to attract any response. He was standing south at the time, the wind being well in the north-east; and Martin Alonso Pinzon, whose caravel pointed into the wind much better than the unhandy Santa Maria, was standing to the east. When evening fell he was still in sight, at a distance of sixteen miles. Columbus was really concerned, and fired lombards and flew more signals of invitation; but there was no reply. In the evening he shortened sail and burned a torch all night, "because it appeared that Martin Alonso was returning to me; and the night was very clear, and there was a nice little breeze by which to come to me if he wished." But he did not wish, and he did not come.

Martin Alonso has in fact shown himself at last in his true colours. He has got the fastest ship, he has got a picked company of his own men from Palos; he has got an Indian on board, moreover, who has guaranteed to take him straight to where the gold is; and he has a very agreeable plan of going and getting it, and returning to Spain with the first news and the first wealth. It is open mutiny, and as such cannot but be a matter of serious regret and trouble to the Admiral, who sits writing up his Journal by the swinging lamp in his little cabin. To that friend and confidant he pours out his troubles and his long list of grievances against Martin Alonso; adding, "He has done and said many other things to me." Up on deck the torch is burning to light the wanderer back again, if only he will come; and there is "a nice little breeze" by which to come if he wishes; but Martin Alonso has wishes quite other than that.

The Pinta was out of sight the next morning, and the little Nina was all that the Admiral had to rely upon for convoy. They were now near the east end of the north coast of Cuba, and they stood in to a harbour which the Admiral called Santa Catalina, and which is now called Cayo de Moa. As the importance of the Nina to the expedition had been greatly increased by the defection of the Pinta, Columbus went on board and examined her. He found that some of her spars were in danger of giving way; and as there was a forest of pine trees rising from the shore he was able to procure a new mizzen mast and latine yard in case it should be necessary to replace those of the Nina. The next morning he weighed anchor at sunrise and continued east along the coast. He had now arrived at the extreme end of Cuba, and was puzzled as to what course he should take. Believing Cuba, as he did, to be the mainland of Cathay, he would have liked to follow the coast in its trend to the south-west, in the hope of coming upon the rich city of Quinsay; but on the other hand there was looming to the south-west some land which the natives with him assured him was Bohio, the place where all the gold was. He therefore held on his course; but when the Indians found that he was really going to these islands they became very much alarmed, and made signs that the people would eat them if they went there; and, in order further to dissuade the Admiral, they added that the people there had only one eye, and the faces, of dogs. As it did not suit Columbus to believe them he said that they were lying, and that he "felt" that the island must belong to the domain of the Great Khan. He therefore continued his course, seeing many beautiful and enchanting bays opening before him, and longing to go into them, but heroically stifling his curiosity, "because he was detained more than he desired by the pleasure and delight he felt in seeing and gazing on the beauty and freshness of those countries wherever he entered, and because he did not wish to be delayed in prosecuting what he was engaged upon; and for these reasons he remained that night beating about and standing off and on until day." He could not trust himself, that is to say, to anchor in these beautiful harbours, for he knew he would be tempted to go ashore and waste valuable time exploring the woods; and so he remained instead, beating about in the open sea.

As it was, what with contrary winds and his own indecision as to which course he should pursue, it was December the 6th before he came up with the beautiful island of Hayti, and having sent the Nina in front to explore for a harbour, entered the Mole Saint Nicholas, which he called Puerto Maria. Towards the east he saw an island shaped like a turtle, and this island he named Tortuga; and the harbour, which he entered that evening on the hour of Vespers, he called Saint Nicholas, as it was the feast of that saint. Once more his description flounders among superlatives: he thought Cuba was perfect; but he finds the new island more perfect still. The climate is like May in Cordova; the tracts of arable land and fertile valleys and high mountains are like those in Castile; he finds mullet like those of Castile; soles and other fish like those in Castile; nightingales and other small birds like those in Castile; myrtle and other trees and grasses like those in Castile! In short, this new land is so like Spain, only more wonderful and beautiful, that he christens it Espanola.

They stayed two days in the harbour of Saint Nicholas, and then began to coast eastwards along the shores of Espaniola. Their best progress was made at dawn and sunset, when the land breeze blew off the island; and during the day they encountered a good deal of colder weather and easterly winds, which made their progress slow. Every day they put in at one or other of the natural harbours in which that beautiful coast abounds; every day they saw natives on the shores who generally fled at their approach, but were often prevailed upon to return and to converse with the natives on board the Admiral's ship, and to receive presents and bring parrots and bits of gold in exchange. On one day a party of men foraging ashore saw a beautiful young girl, who fled at their approach; and they chased her a long way through the woods, finally capturing her and bringing her on board. Columbus "caused her to be clothed" —doubtless a diverting occupation for Rodrigo, Juan, Garcia, Pedro, William, and the rest of them, although for the poor, shy, trembling captive not diverting at all— and sent her ashore again loaded with beads and brass rings—to act as a decoy. Having sown this good seed the Admiral waited for a night, and then sent a party of men ashore, "well prepared with arms and adapted for such an affair," to have some conversation with the people. The innocent harvest was duly reaped; the natives met the Spaniards with gifts of food and drink, and understanding that the Admiral would like to have a parrot, they sent as many parrots as were wanted. The husband of the girl who had been captured and clothed came back with her to the shore with a large body of natives, in order to thank the Admiral for his kindness and clemency; and their confidence was not misplaced, as the Admiral did not at that moment wish to do any more kidnapping. The Spaniards were more and more amazed and impressed with the beauty and fertility of these islands. The lands were more lovely than the finest land in Castile; the rivers were large and wide, the trees green and full of fruit, the grasses knee-deep and starred with flowers; the birds sang sweetly all night; there were mastic trees and aloes and plantations of cotton. There was fishing in plenty; and if there were not any gold mines immediately at hand, they here sure to be round the next headland or, at the farthest, in the next island. The people, too, charmed and delighted the Admiral, who saw in them a future glorious army of souls converted to the Christian religion. They were taller and handsomer than the inhabitants of the other islands, and the women much fairer; indeed, if they had not been so much exposed to the sun, and if they could only be clothed in the decent garments of civilisation, the Admiral thought that their skins would be as white as those of the women of Spain—which was only another argument for bringing them within the fold of the Holy Catholic Church. The men were powerful and apparently harmless; they showed no truculent or suspicious spirit; they had no knowledge of arms; a thousand of them would not face three Christians; and

"so they are suitable to be governed and made to work and sow and do everything else that shall be necessary, and to build villages and be taught to wear clothing and observe our customs."

At present, you see, they are but poor happy heathens, living in a paradise of their own, where the little birds sing all through the warm nights, and the rivers murmur through flowery meadows, and no one has any knowledge of arms or desire of such knowledge, and every one goes naked and unashamed. High time, indeed, that they should be taught to wear clothing and observe our customs.

The local chief came on a visit of state to the ship; and the Admiral paid him due honour, telling him that he came as an envoy from the greatest sovereigns in the world. But this charming king, or cacique as they called him, would not believe this; he thought that Columbus was, for reasons of modesty, speaking less than the truth—a new charge to bring against our Christopher! He believed that the Spaniards came from heaven, and that the realms of the sovereigns of Castile were in the heavens and not in this world. He took some refreshment, as his councillors did also, little dreaming, poor wretches, what in after years was to come to them through all this palavering and exchanging of presents. The immediate result of the interview, however, was to make intercourse with the natives much freer and pleasanter even than it had been before; and some of the sailors went fishing with the natives. It was then that they were shown some cane arrows with hardened points, which the natives said belonged to the people of 'Caniba', who, they alleged, came to the island to capture and eat the natives. The Admiral did not believe it; his sublime habit of rejecting everything that did not fit in with his theory of the moment, and accepting everything that did, made him shake his head when this piece of news was brought to him. He could not get the Great Khan out of his head, and his present theory was that this island, being close to the mainland of Cathay, was visited by the armies of the Great Khan, and that it was his men who had used the arrows and made war upon the natives. It was no good for the natives to show him some of their mutilated bodies, and to tell him that the cannibals ate them piecemeal; he had no use for such information. His mind was like a sieve of which the size of the meshes could be adjusted at will; everything that was not germane to the idea of the moment fell through it, and only confirmative evidence remained; and at the moment he was not believing any stories which did not prove that the Great Khan was, so to speak, just round the corner. If they talked about gold he would listen to them; and so the cacique brought him a piece of gold the size of his hand and, breaking it into pieces, gave it to him a bit at a time. This the Admiral took to be sign of great intelligence. They told him there was gold at Tortuga, but he preferred to believe that it came from Babeque, which may have been Jamaica and may have been nothing at all.

But his theory was that it existed on Espanola only in small pieces because that country was so rich that the natives had no need for it; an economic theory which one grows dizzy in pondering. At any rate "the Admiral believed that he was very near the fountainhead, and that Our Lord was about to show him where the gold originates."

On Tuesday, December 18th, the ships were all dressed in honour of a religious anniversary, and the cacique, hearing the firing of the lombards with which the festival was greeted, came down to the shore to see what was the matter. As Columbus was sitting at dinner on deck beneath the poop the cacique arrived with all his people; and the account of his visit is preserved in Columbus's own words.

"As he entered the ship he found that I was eating at the table below the stern forecastle, and he came quickly to seat himself beside me, and would not allow me to go to meet him or get up from the table, but only that I should eat. I thought that he would like to eat some of our viands and I then ordered that things should be brought him to eat. And when he entered under the forecastle, he signed with his hand that all his people should remain without, and they did so with the greatest haste and respect in the world, and all seated themselves on the deck, except two men of mature age whom I took to be his counsellors and governors, and who came and seated themselves at his feet: and of the viands which I placed before him he took of each one as much as may be taken for a salutation, and then he sent the rest to his people and they all ate some of it, and he did the same with the drink, which he only touched to his mouth, and then gave it to the others in the same way, and it was all done in wonderful state and with very few words, and whatever he said, according to what I was able to understand, was very formal and prudent, and those two looked in his face and spoke for him and with him, and with great respect.

"After eating, a page brought a belt which is like those of Castile in shape, but of a different make, which he took and gave me, and also two wrought pieces of gold, which were very thin, as I believe they obtain very little of it here, although I consider they are very near the place where it has its home, and that there is a great deal of it. I saw that a drapery that I had upon my bed pleased him. I gave it to him, and some very good amber beads which I wore around my neck and some red shoes and a flask of orange-flower water, with which he was so pleased it was wonderful; and he and his governor and counsellors were very sorry that they did not understand me, nor I them. Nevertheless I understood that he told me that if anything from here would satisfy me that all the island was at my command. I sent for some beads of mine, where as a sign I have a 'excelente' of gold upon which the images of your Highnesses are engraved, and showed it to him, and again told him the same as yesterday, that your Highnesses command and rule over all the best part of the world, and that there are no other such great Princes: and I showed him the royal banners and the others with the cross, which he held in great estimation: and he said to his counsellors that your Highnesses must be great Lords, since you had sent me here from so far without fear: and many other things happened which I did not understand, except that I very well saw he considered everything as very wonderful."

Later in the day Columbus got into talk with an old man who told him that there was a great quantity of gold to be found on some island about a hundred leagues away; that there was one island that was all gold; and that in the others there was such a quantity that they natives gathered it and sifted it with sieves and made it into bars. The old man pointed out vaguely the direction in which this wonderful country lay; and if he had not been one of the principal persons belonging to the King Columbus would have detained him and taken him with him; but he decided that he had paid the cacique too much respect to make it right that he should kidnap one of his retinue. He determined, however, to go and look for the gold. Before he left he had a great cross erected in the middle of the Indian village; and as he made sail out of the harbour that evening he could see the Indians kneeling round the cross and adoring it. He sailed eastward, anchoring for a day in the Bay of Acul, which he called Cabo de Caribata, receiving something like an ovation from the natives, and making them presents and behaving very graciously and kindly to them.

It was at this time that Columbus made the acquaintance of a man whose character shines like a jewel amid the dismal scenes that afterwards accompanied the first bursting of the wave of civilisation on these happy shores. This was the king of that part of the island, a young man named Guacanagari. This king sent out a large canoe full of people to the Admiral's ship, with a request that Columbus would land in his country, and a promise that the chief would give him whatever he had. There must have been an Intelligence Department in the island, for the chief seemed to know what would be most likely to attract the Admiral; and with his messengers he sent out a belt with a large golden mask attached to it. Unfortunately the natives on board the Admiral's ship could not understand Guacanagari's messengers, and nearly the whole of the day was passed in talking before the sense of their message was finally made out by means of signs. In the evening some Spaniards were sent ashore to see if they could not get some gold; but Columbus, who had evidently had some recent experience of their avariciousness, and who was anxious to keep on good terms with the chiefs of the island, sent his secretary with them to see that they did nothing unjust or unreasonable. He was scrupulous to see that the natives got their bits of glass and beads in exchange for the gold; and it is due to him to remember that now, as always, he was rigid in regulating his conduct with other men in accordance with his ideas of justice and honour, however elastic those ideas may seem to have been. The ruffianly crew had in their minds only the immediate possession of what they could get from the Indians; the Admiral had in his mind the whole possession of the islands and the bodies and souls of its inhabitants. If you take a piece of gold without giving a glass bead in exchange for it, it is called stealing; if you take a country and its inhabitants, and steal their peace from them, and give them blood and servitude in exchange for it, it is called colonisation and Empire-building. Every one understands the distinction; but so few people see the difference that Columbus of all men may be excused for his unconsciousness of it.

Indeed Columbus was seeing yellow at this point in his career. The word "gold" is scattered throughout every page of his journal; he can understand nothing that the natives say to him except that there is a great quantity of gold somewhere about. He is surrounded by natives pressing presents upon him, protesting their homage, and assuring him (so he thinks) that there are any amount of gold mines; and no wonder that the yellow light blinds his eyes and confounds his senses, and that sometimes, even when the sun has gone down and the natives have retired to their villages and he sits alone in the seclusion of his cabin, the glittering motes still dance before his eyes and he becomes mad, maudlin, ecstatic . . . . The light flickers in the lamp as the ship swings a little on the quiet tide and a night breeze steals through the cabin door; the sound of voices ashore sounds dimly across the water; the brain of the Admiral, overfilled with wonders and promises and hopes, sends its message to the trembling hand that holds the pen, and the incoherent words stream out on the ink. "May our Lord in His mercy direct me until I find this gold, I say this Mine, because I have many people here who say that they know it."

On Christmas Eve a serious misfortune befell Columbus. What with looking for gold, and trying to understand the people who talked about it, and looking after his ships, and writing up his journal, he had had practically no sleep for two days and a night; and at eleven o'clock on the 24th of December, the night being fine and his ship sailing along the coast with a light land breeze, he decided to lie down to get some sleep. There were no difficulties in navigation to be feared, because the ship's boats had been rowed the day before a distance of about ten miles ahead on the course which they were then steering and had seen that there was open water all the way. The wind fell calm; and the man at the helm, having nothing to do, and feeling sleepy, called a ship's boy to him, gave him the helm, and went off himself to lie down. This of course was against all rules; but as the Admiral was in his cabin and there was no one to tell them otherwise the watch on deck thought it a very good opportunity to rest. Suddenly the boy felt the rudder catch upon something, saw the ship swinging, and immediately afterwards heard the sound of tide ripples. He cried out; and in a moment Columbus, who was sleeping the light sleep of an anxious shipmaster, came tumbling up to see what was the matter. The current, which flows in that place at a speed of about two knots, had carried the ship on to a sand bank, but she touched so quietly that it was hardly felt. Close on the heels of, Columbus came the master of the ship and the delinquent watch; and the Admiral immediately ordered them to launch the ship's boat—and lay out an anchor astern so that they could warp her off. The wretches lowered the boat, but instead of getting the anchor on board rowed off in the direction of the Nina, which was lying a mile and a half to windward. As soon as Columbus saw what they were doing he ran to the side and, seeing that the tide was failing and that the ship had swung round across the bank, ordered the remainder of the crew to cut away the mainmast and throw the deck hamper overboard, in order to lighten the ship. This took some time; the tide was falling, and the ship beginning to heel over on her beam; and by the time it was done the Admiral saw that it would be of no use, for the ship's seams had opened and she was filling.

At this point the miserable crew in the ship's boat came back, the loyal people on the Nina having refused to receive them and sent them back to the assistance of the Admiral. But it was now too late to do anything to save the ship; and as he did not know but that she might break up, Columbus decided to tranship the people to the Nina, who had by this time sent her own boat. The whole company boarded the Nina, on which the Admiral beat about miserably till morning in the vicinity of his doomed ship. Then he sent Diego de Arana, the brother of Beatriz and a trusty friend, ashore in a boat to beg the help of the King; and Guacanagari immediately sent his people with large canoes to unload the wrecked ship, which was done with great efficiency and despatch, and the whole of her cargo and fittings stored on shore under a guard. And so farewell to the Santa Maria, whose bones were thenceforward to bleach upon the shores of Hayti, or incongruously adorn the dwellings of the natives. She may have been "a bad sailer and unfit for discovery"; but no seaman looks without emotion upon the wreck of a ship whose stem has cut the waters of home, which has carried him safely over thousands of uncharted miles, and which has for so long been his shelter and sanctuary.

At sunrise the kind-hearted cacique came down to the Nina, where Columbus had taken up his quarters, and with tears in his eyes begged the Admiral not to grieve at his losses, for that he, the cacique, would give him everything that he possessed; that he had already given two large houses to the Spaniards from the Santa Maria who had been obliged to encamp on shore, and that he would provide more accommodation and help if necessary. In fact, the day which had been ushered in so disastrously turned into a very happy one; and before it was over Columbus had decided that, as he could not take the whole of his company home on the Nina, he would establish a settlement on shore so that the men who were left behind could collect gold and store it until more ships could be sent from Spain. The natives came buzzing round anxious to barter whatever they had for hawks' bells, which apparently were the most popular of the toys that had been brought for bartering; "they shouted and showed the pieces of gold, saying chuq, chuq, for hawks' bells, as they are in a likely state to become crazy for them." The cacique was delighted to see that the Admiral was pleased with the gold that was brought to him, and he cheered him up by telling him that there was any amount in Cibao, which Columbus of course took for Cipango. The cacique entertained Columbus to a repast on shore, at which the monarch wore a shirt and a pair of gloves that Columbus had given him; "and he rejoiced more over the gloves than anything that had been given him." Columbus was pleased with his clean and leisurely method of eating, and with his dainty rubbing of his hands with herbs after he had eaten. After the repast Columbus gave a little demonstration of bow-and-arrow shooting and the firing of lombards and muskets, all of which astonished and impressed the natives.

The afternoon was spent in deciding on a site for the fortress which was to be constructed; and Columbus had no difficulty in finding volunteers among the crews to remain in the settlement. He promised to leave with them provisions of bread and wine for a year, a ship's boat, seeds for sowing crops, and a carpenter, a caulker, a gunner, and a cooper. Before the day was out he was already figuring up the profit that would arise out of his misfortune of the day before; and he decided that it was the act of God which had cast his ship away in order that this settlement should be founded. He hoped that the settlers would have a ton of gold ready for him when he came back from Castile, so that, as he had said in the glittering camp of Santa Fe, where perhaps no one paid very much heed to him, there might be such a profit as would provide for the conquest of Jerusalem and the recovery of the Holy Sepulchre. After all, if he was greedy for gold, he had a pious purpose for its employment.

The last days of the year were very busy ones for the members of the expedition. Assisted by the natives they were building the fort which, in memory of the day on which it was founded, Columbus called La Villa-de la Navidad. The Admiral spent much time with King Guacanagari, who "loved him so much that it was wonderful," and wished to cover him all over with gold before he went away, and begged him not to go before it was done. On December 27th there was some good news; a caravel had been seen entering a harbour a little further along the coast; and as this could only mean that the Pinta had returned, Columbus borrowed a canoe from the king, and despatched a sailor in it to carry news of his whereabouts to the Pinta. While it was away Guacanagari collected all the other kings and chiefs who were subject to him, and held a kind of durbar. They all wore their crowns; and Guacanagari took off his crown and placed it on Columbus's head; and the Admiral, not to be outdone, took from his own neck "a collar of good bloodstones and very beautiful beads of fine colours; which appeared very good in all parts, and placed it upon the King; and he took off a cloak of fine scarlet cloth which he had put on that day, and clothed the King with it; and he sent for some coloured buskins which he made him put on, and placed upon his finger a large silver ring"—all of which gives us a picturesque glimpse into the contents of the Admiral's wardrobe, and a very agreeable picture of King Guacanagari, whom we must now figure as clothed, in addition to his shirt and gloves, in a pair of coloured buskins, a collar of bloodstones, a scarlet cloak and a silver ring.

But the time was running short; the Admiral, hampered as he was by the possession of only one small ship, had now but one idea, which was to get back to Castile as quickly as possible, report the result of his discoveries, and come back again with a larger and more efficient equipment. Before he departed he had an affectionate leave-taking with King Guacanagari; he gave him another shirt, and also provided a demonstration of the effect of lombards by having one loaded, and firing at the old Santa Maria where she lay hove down on the sandbank. The shot went clean through her hull and fell into the sea beyond, and produced what might be called a very strong moral effect, although an unnecessary one, on the natives. He then set about the very delicate business of organising the settlement. In all, forty-two men were to remain behind, with Diego de Arana in the responsible position of chief lieutenant, assisted by Pedro Gutierrez and Rodrigo de Escovedo, the nephew of Friar Juan Perez of La Rabida. To these three he delegated all his powers and authority as Admiral and Viceroy; and then, having collected the colonists, gave them a solemn address. First, he reminded them of the goodness of God to them, and advised them to remain worthy of it by obeying the Divine command in all their actions. Second, he ordered them, as a representative of the Sovereigns of Spain, to obey the captain whom he had appointed for them as they would have obeyed himself. Third, he urged them to show respect and reverence towards King Guacanagari and his chiefs, and to the inferior chiefs, and to avoid annoying them or tormenting them, since they were to remain in a land that was as yet under native dominion; to "strive and watch by their soft and honest speech to gain their good-will and keep their friendship and love, so that he should find them as friendly and favourable and more so when he returned." Fourth, he commanded them "and begged them earnestly" to do no injury and use no force against any natives; to take nothing from them against their will; and especially to be on their guard to avoid injury or violence to the women, "by which they would cause scandal and set a bad example to the Indians and show the infamy of the Christians." Fifth, he charged them not to scatter themselves or leave the place where they then were, but to remain together until he returned. Sixth, he "animated" them to suffer their solitude and exile cheerfully and bravely, since they had willingly chosen it. The seventh order was, that they should get help from the King to send boat expeditions in search of the gold mines; and lastly, he promised that he would petition the Sovereigns to honour them with special favours and rewards. To this very manly, wise and humane address the people listened with some emotion, assuring Columbus that they placed their hopes in him, "begging him earnestly to remember them always, and that as quickly as he could he should give them the great joy which they anticipated from his coming again."

All of which things being done, the ships [ship—there was only the Nina] loaded and provisioned, and the Admiral's final directions given, he makes his farewells and weighs anchor at sunrise on Friday, January 4., 1493. Among the little crowd on the shore who watch the Nina growing smaller in the distance are our old friends Allard and William, tired of the crazy confinement of a ship and anxious for shore adventures. They are to have their fill of them, as it happens; adventures that are to bring to the settlers a sudden cloud of blood and darkness, and for the islanders a brief return to their ancient peace. But death waits for Allard and William in the sunshine and silence of Espanola.

CHAPTER III

THE VOYAGE HOME

Columbus did not stand out to sea on his homeward course immediately, but still coasted along the shores of the island as though he were loth to leave it, and as though he might still at some bend of a bay or beyond some verdant headland come upon the mines and jewels that he longed for. The mountain that he passed soon after starting he called Monte Christi, which name it bears to this day; and he saw many other mountains and capes and bays, to all of which he gave names. And it was a fortunate chance which led him thus to stand along the coast of the island; for on January 6th the sailor who was at the masthead, looking into the clear water for shoals and rocks, reported that he saw the caravel Pinta right ahead. When she came up with him, as they were in very shallow water not suitable for anchorage, Columbus returned to the bay of Monte Christi to anchor there. Presently Martin Alonso Pinzon came on board to report himself—a somewhat crestfallen Martin, we may be sure, for he had failed to find the gold the hope of which had led him to break his honour as a seaman. But the Martin Alonsos of this world, however sorry their position may be, will always find some kind of justification for it. It must have been a trying moment for Martin Alonso as his boat from the Pinta drew near the Nina, and he saw the stalwart commanding figure of the white-haired Admiral walking the poop. He knew very well that according to the law and custom of the sea Columbus would have been well within his right in shooting him or hanging him on the spot; but Martin puts on a bold face as, with a cold dread at his heart and (as likely as not) an ingratiating smile upon his face he comes up over the side. Perhaps, being in some ways a cleverer man than Christopher, he knew the Admiral's weak points; knew that he was kind-hearted, and would remember those days of preparation at Palos when Martin Alonso had been his principal stay and help. Martin's story was that he had been separated from the Admiral against his will; that the crew insisted upon it, and that in any case they had only meant to go and find some gold and bring it back to the Admiral. Columbus did not believe him for a moment, but either his wisdom or his weakness prevented him from saying so. He reproached Martin Alonso for acting with pride and covetousness "that night when he went away and left him"; and Columbus could not think "from whence had come the haughty actions and dishonesty Martin had shown towards him on that voyage." Martin had done a good trade and had got a certain amount of gold; and no doubt he knew well in what direction to turn the conversation when it was becoming unpleasant to himself. He told Columbus of an island to the south of Juana—[Cuba]—called Yamaye,—

[Jamaica]—where pieces of gold were taken from the mines as large as kernels of wheat, and of another island towards the east which was inhabited only by women.

The unpleasantness was passed over as soon as possible, although the Admiral felt that the sooner he got home the better, since he was practically at the mercy of the Pinzon brothers and their following from Palos. He therefore had the Pinta beached and recaulked and took in wood and water, and continued his voyage on Tuesday, January 8th. He says that "this night in the name of our Lord he will start on his journey without delaying himself further for any matter, since he had found what he had sought, and he did not wish to have more trouble with that Martin Alonso until their Highnesses learned the news of the voyage and what he has done." After that it will be another matter, and his turn will come; for then, he says, "I will not suffer the bad deeds of persons without virtue, who, with little respect, presume to carry out their own wills in opposition to those who did them honour." Indeed, for several days, the name of "that Martin Alonso" takes the place of gold in Columbus's Journal. There were all kinds of gossip about the ill deeds of Martin Alonso, who had taken four Indian men and two young girls by force; the Admiral releasing them immediately and sending them back to their homes. Martin Alonso, moreover, had made a rule that half the gold that was found was to be kept by himself; and he tried to get all the people of his ship to swear that he had been trading for only six days, but "his wickedness was so public that he could not hide it." It was a good thing that Columbus had his journal to talk to, for he worked off a deal of bitterness in it. On Sunday, January 13th, when he had sent a boat ashore to collect some "ajes" or potatoes, a party of natives with their faces painted and with the plumes of parrots in their hair came and attacked the party from the boat; but on getting a slash or two with a cutlass they took to flight and escaped from the anger of the Spaniards. Columbus thought that they were cannibals or caribs, and would like to have taken some of them, but they did not come back, although afterwards he collected four youths who came out to the caravel with cotton and arrows.

Columbus was very curious about the island of Matinino,—[Martinique] —which was the one said to be inhabited only by women, and he wished very much to go there; but the caravels were leaking badly, the crews were complaining, and he was reluctantly compelled to shape his course for Spain. He sailed to the north-east, being anxious apparently to get into the region of westerly winds which he correctly guessed would be found to the north of the course he had sailed on his outward voyage. By the 17th of January he was in the vicinity of the Sargasso Sea again, which this time had no terrors for him. From his journal the word "gold" suddenly disappears; the Viceroy and Governor-General steps off the stage; and in his place appears the sea captain, watching the frigate birds and pelicans, noting the golden gulf-weed in the sea, and smelling the breezes that are once more as sweet as the breezes of Seville in May. He had a good deal of trouble with his dead-reckoning at this time, owing to the changing winds and currents; but he made always from fifty to seventy miles a day in a direction between north-by-east and north-north-east. The Pinta was not sailing well, and he often had to wait for her to come up with him; and he reflected in his journal that if Martin Alonso Pinzon had taken as much pains to provide himself with a good mast in the Indies as he had to separate himself from the Admiral, the Pinta would have sailed better.

And so he went on for several days, with the wind veering always south and south-west, and pointing pretty steadily to the north-east. On February 4th he changed his course, and went as near due east as he could. They now began to find themselves in considerable doubt as to their position. The Admiral said he was seventy-five leagues to the south of Flores; Vincenti Pinzon and the pilots thought that they had passed the Azores and were in the neighbourhood of Madeira. In other words, there was a difference of 600 miles between their estimates, and the Admiral remarks that "the grace of God permitting, as soon as land is seen, it will be known who has calculated the surest."

A great quantity of birds that began to fly about the ship made him think that they were near land, but they turned out to be the harbingers of a storm. On Tuesday, February 12th, the sea and wind began to rise, and it continued to blow harder throughout that night and the next day. The wind being aft he went under bare poles most of the night, and when day came hoisted a little sail; but the sea was terrible, and if he had not been so sure of the staunch little Nina he would have felt himself in danger of being lost. The next day the sea, instead of going down, increased in roughness; there was a heavy cross sea which kept breaking right over the ship, and it became necessary to make a little sail in order to run before the wind, and to prevent the vessel falling back into the trough of the seas. All through Thursday he ran thus under the half hoisted staysail, and he could see the Pinta running also before the wind, although since she presented more surface, and was able to carry a little more sail than the Nina, she was soon lost to sight. The Admiral showed lights through the night, and this time there was no lack of response from Martin Alonso; and for some part of that dark and stormy night these two humanly freighted scraps of wood and cordage staggered through the gale showing lights to each other; until at last the light from the Pinta disappeared. When morning came she was no longer to be seen; and the wind and the sea had if anything increased. The Nina was now in the greatest danger. Any one wave of the heavy cross sea, if it had broken fairly across her, would have sunk her; and she went swinging and staggering down into the great valleys and up into the hills, the steersman's heart in his mouth, and the whole crew in an extremity of fear. Columbus, who generally relied upon his seamanship, here invoked external aid, and began to offer bargains to the Almighty. He ordered that lots should be cast, and that he upon whom the lot fell should make a vow to go on pilgrimage to Santa Maria de Guadaloupe carrying a white candle of five pounds weight. Same dried peas were brought, one for every member of the crew, and on one of them a cross was marked with a knife; the peas were well shaken and were put into a cap. The first to draw was the Admiral; he drew the marked pea, and he made the vow. Lots were again drawn, this time for a greater pilgrimage to Santa Maria de Loretto in Ancona; and the lot fell on a seaman named Pedro de Villa, —the expenses of whose pilgrimage Columbus promised to pay. Again lots were drawn for a pilgrimage to the shrine of Santa Clara of Moguer, the pilgrim to watch and pray for one night there; and again the lot fell on Columbus. In addition to these, every one, since they took themselves for lost, made some special and private vow or bargain with God; and finally they all made a vow together that at the first land they reached they would go in procession in their shirts to pray at an altar of Our Lady.

The scene thus conjured up is one peculiar to the time and condition of these people, and is eloquent and pathetic enough: the little ship staggering and bounding along before the wind, and the frightened crew, who had gone through so many other dangers, huddled together under the forecastle, drawing peas out of a cap, crossing themselves, making vows upon their knees, and seeking to hire the protection of the Virgin by their offers of candles and pilgrimages. Poor Christopher, standing in his drenched oilskins and clinging to a piece of rigging, had his own searching of heart and examining of conscience. He was aware of the feverish anxiety and impatience that he felt, now that he had been successful in discovering a New World, to bring home the news and fruits of it; his desire to prove true what he had promised was so great that, in his own graphic phrase, "it seemed to him that every gnat could disturb and impede it"; and he attributed this anxiety to his lack of faith in God. He comforted himself, like Robinson Crusoe in a similar extremity, by considering on the other hand what favours God had shown him, and by remembering that it was to the glory of God that the fruits of his discovery were to be dedicated. But in the meantime here he was in a ship insufficiently ballasted (for she was now practically empty of provisions, and they had found it necessary to fill the wine and water casks with salt water in order to trim her) and flying before a tempest such as he had never experienced in his life. As a last resource, and in order to give his wonderful news a chance of reaching Spain in case the ship were lost, he went into his cabin and somehow or other managed to write on a piece of parchment a brief account of his discoveries, begging any one who might find it to carry it to the Spanish Sovereigns. He tied up the parchment in a waxed cloth, and put it into a large barrel without any one seeing him, and then ordered the barrel to be thrown into the sea, which the crew took to be some pious act of sacrifice or devotion. Then he went back on deck and watched the last of the daylight going and the green seas swelling and thundering about his little ship, and thought anxiously of his two little boys at school in Cordova, and wondered what would become of them if he were lost. The next morning the wind had changed a little, though it was still very high; but he was able to hoist up the bonnet or topsail, and presently the sea began to go down a little. When the sun rose they saw land to the east-north-east. Some of them thought it was Madeira, others the rock of Cintra in Portugal; the pilots said it was the coast of Spain, the Admiral thought it was the Azores; but at any rate it was land of some kind. The sun was shining upon it and upon the tumbling sea; and although the waves were still raging mast-high and the wind still blowing a hard gale, the miserable crew were able to hope that, having lived through the night, they could live through the day also. They had to beat about to make the land, which was now ahead of them, now on the beam, and now astern; and although they had first sighted it at sunrise on Friday morning it was early on Monday morning, February 18th, before Columbus was able to cast anchor off the northern coast of an island which he discovered to be the island of Santa Maria in the Azores. On this day Columbus found time to write a letter to Luis de Santangel, the royal Treasurer, giving a full account of his voyage and discoveries; which letter he kept and despatched on the 4th of March, after he had arrived in Lisbon. Since it contained a postscript written at the last moment we shall read it at that stage of our narrative. The inhabitants of Santa Maria received the voyagers with astonishment, for they believed that nothing could have lived through the tempest that had been raging for the last fortnight. They were greatly excited by the story of the discoveries; and the Admiral, who had now quite recovered command of himself, was able to pride himself on the truth of his dead-reckoning, which had proved to be so much more accurate than that of the pilots.

On the Tuesday evening three men hailed them from the shore, and when they were brought off to the ship delivered a message from the Portuguese Governor of the island, Juan de Castaneda, to the effect that he knew the Admiral very well, and that he was delighted to hear of his wonderful voyage. The next morning Columbus, remembering the vow that had been made in the storm, sent half the crew ashore in their shirts to a little hermitage, which was on the other side of a point a short distance away, and asked the Portuguese messenger to send a priest to say Mass for them. While the members of the crew were at their prayers, however, they received a rude surprise. They were suddenly attacked by the islanders, who had come up on horses under the command of the treacherous Governor, and taken prisoners. Columbus waited unsuspectingly for the boat to come back with them, in order that he and the other half of the crew could go and perform their vow.

When the boat did not come back he began to fear that some accident must have happened to it, and getting his anchor up he set sail for the point beyond which the hermitage was situated. No sooner had he rounded the point than he saw a band of horsemen, who dismounted, launched the boat which was drawn up on the beach, and began to row out, evidently with the intention of attacking the Admiral. When they came up to the Nina the man in command of them rose and asked Columbus to assure him of personal safety; which assurance was wonderingly given; and the Admiral inquired how it was that none of his own people were in the boat? Columbus suspected treachery and tried to meet it with treachery also, endeavouring with smooth words to get the captain to come on board so that he could seize him as a hostage. But as the Portuguese would not come on board Columbus told them that they were acting very unwisely in affronting his people; that in the land of the Sovereigns of Castile the Portuguese were treated with great honour and security; that he held letters of recommendation from the Sovereigns addressed to every ruler in the world, and added that he was their Admiral of the Ocean Seas and Viceroy of the Indies, and could show the Portuguese his commission to that effect; and finally, that if his people were not returned to him, he would immediately make sail for Spain with the crew that was left to him and report this insult to the Spanish Sovereigns. To all of which the Portuguese captain replied that he did not know any Sovereigns of Castile; that neither they nor their letters were of any account in that island; that they were not afraid of Columbus; and that they would have him know that he had Portugal to deal with—edging away in the boat at the same time to a convenient distance from the caravel. When he thought he was out of gunshot he shouted to Columbus, ordering him to take his caravel back to the harbour by command of the Governor of the island. Columbus answered by calling his crew to witness that he pledged his word not to descend from or leave his caravel until he had taken a hundred Portuguese to Castile, and had depopulated all their islands. After which explosion of words he returned to the harbour and anchored there, "as the weather and wind were very unfavourable for anything else."

He was, however, in a very bad anchorage, with a rocky bottom which presently fouled his anchors; and on the Wednesday he had to make sail towards the island of San Miguel if order to try and find a better anchorage.

But the wind and sea getting up again very badly he was obliged to beat about all night in a very unpleasant situation, with only three sailors who could be relied upon, and a rabble of gaol-birds and longshoremen who were of little use in a tempest but to draw lots and vow pilgrimages. Finding himself unable to make the island of San Miguel he decided to go back to Santa Maria and make an attempt to recover his boat and his crew and the anchor and cables he had lost there.

In his Journal for this day, and amid all his anxieties, he found time to note down one of his curious visionary cosmographical reflections. This return to a region of storms and heavy seas reminded him of the long months he had spent in the balmy weather and calm waters of his discovery; in which facts he found a confirmation of the theological idea that the Eden, or Paradise, of earth was "at the end of the Orient, because it is a most temperate place. So that these lands which he had now discovered are at the end of the Orient." Reflections such as these, which abound in his writings, ought in themselves to be a sufficient condemnation of those who have endeavoured to prove that Columbus was a man of profound cosmographical learning and of a scientific mind. A man who would believe that he had discovered the Orient because in the place where he had been he had found calm weather, and because the theologians said that the Garden of Eden must be in the Orient since it is a temperate place, would believe anything.

Late on Thursday night, when he anchored again in the harbour of San Lorenzo at Santa Maria, a man hailed them from the rocks, and asked them not to go away. Presently a boat containing five sailors, two priests, and a notary put off from the beach; and they asked for a guarantee of security in order that they might treat with the Admiral. They slept on board that night, and in the morning asked him to show them his authority from the Spanish Sovereigns, which the Admiral did, understanding that they had asked for this formality in order to save their dignity. He showed them his general letter from the King and Queen of Spain, addressed to "Princes and Lords of High Degree"; and being satisfied with this they went ashore and released the Admiral's people, from whom he learned that what had been done had been done by command of the King of Portugal, and that he had issued an order to the Governors of all the Portuguese islands that if Columbus landed there on his way home he was to be taken prisoner.

He sailed again on Sunday, February 24th, encountering heavy winds and seas, which troubled him greatly with fears lest some disaster should happen at the eleventh hour to interfere with his, triumph. On Sunday, March 3rd, the wind rose to the force of a hurricane, and, on a sudden gust of violent wind splitting all the sails, the unhappy crew gathered together again and drew more lots and made more vows. This time the pilgrimage was to be to the shrine of Santa Maria at Huelva, the pilgrim to go as before in his shirt; and the lot fell to the Admiral. The rest of them made a vow to fast on the next Saturday on bread and water; but as they all thought it extremely unlikely that by that time they would be in need of any bodily sustenance the sacrifice could hardly have been a great one. They scudded along under bare poles and in a heavy cross sea all that night; but at dawn on Monday they saw land ahead of them, which Columbus recognised as the rock of Cintra at Lisbon; and at Lisbon sure enough they landed some time during the morning. As soon as they were inside the river the people came flocking down with stories of the gale and of all the wrecks that there had been on the coast. Columbus hurried away from the excited crowds to write a letter to the King of Portugal, asking him for a safe conduct to Spain, and assuring him that he had come from the Indies, and not from any of the forbidden regions of Guinea.

The next day brought a visit from no less a person than Bartholomew Diaz. Columbus had probably met him before in 1486, when Diaz had been a distinguished man and Columbus a man not distinguished; but now things were changed. Diaz ordered Columbus to come on board his small vessel in order to go and report himself to the King's officers; but Columbus replied that he was the Admiral of the Sovereigns of Castile, "that he did not render such account to such persons," and that he declined to leave his ship. Diaz then ordered him to send the captain of the Nina; but Columbus refused to send either the captain or any other person, and otherwise gave himself airs as the Admiral of the Ocean Seas. Diaz then moderated his requests, and merely asked Columbus to show him his letter of authority, which Columbus did; and then Diaz went away and brought back with him the captain of the Portuguese royal yacht, who came in great state on board the shabby little Nina, with kettle-drums and trumpets and pipes, and placed himself at the disposal of Columbus. It is a curious moment, this, in which the two great discoverers of their time, Diaz and Columbus, meet for an hour on the deck of a forty-ton caravel; a curious thing to consider that they who had performed such great feats of skill and bravery, one to discover the southernmost point of the old world and the other to voyage across an uncharted ocean to the discovery of an entirely new world, could find nothing better to talk about than their respective ranks and glories; and found no more interesting subject of discussion than the exact amount of state and privilege which should be accorded to each.

During the day or two in which Columbus waited in the port crowds of people came down from Lisbon to see the little Nina, which was an object of much admiration and astonishment; to see the Indians also, at whom they greatly marvelled. It was probably at this time that the letter addressed to Luis de Santangel, containing the first official account of the voyage, was despatched.

*

*****

*

*

"Sir: As I am sure you will be pleased at the great victory which the Lord has given me in my voyage, I write this to inform you that in twenty' days I arrived in the Indies with the squadron which their Majesties had placed under my command. There I discovered many islands, inhabited by a numerous population, and took possession of them for their Highnesses, with public ceremony and the royal flag displayed, without molestation.

"The first that I discovered I named San Salvador, in remembrance of that Almighty Power which had so miraculously bestowed them. The Indians call it Guanahani. To the second I assigned the name of Santa Marie de Conception; to the third that of Fernandina; to the fourth that of Isabella; to the fifth Juana; and so on, to every one a new name.

"When I arrived at Juana, I followed the coast to the westward, and found it so extensive that I considered it must be a continent and a province of Cathay. And as I found no towns or villages by the seaside, excepting some small settlements, with the people of which I could not communicate because they all ran away, I continued my course to the westward, thinking I should not fail to find some large town and cities. After having coasted many leagues without finding any signs of them, and seeing that the coast took me to the northward, where I did not wish to go, as the winter was already set in, I considered it best to follow the coast to the south and the wind being also scant, I determined to lose no more time, and therefore returned to a certain port, from whence I sent two messengers into the country to ascertain whether there was any king there or any large city.

"They travelled for three days, finding an infinite number of small settlements and an innumerable population, but nothing like a city: on which account—they returned. I had tolerably well ascertained from some Indians whom I had taken that this land was only an island, so I followed the coast of it to the east 107 leagues, to its termination. And about eighteen leagues from this cape, to the east, there was another

35

island, to which I shortly gave the name of Espanola. I went to it, and followed the north coast of it, as I had done that of Juana, for 178—[should be 188]—long leagues due east.

"This island is very fertile, as well, indeed, as all the rest. It possesses numerous harbours, far superior to any I know in Europe, and what is remarkable, plenty of large inlets. The land is high, and contains many lofty ridges and some very high mountains, without comparison of the island of Centrefrey;—[Tenerife]—all of them very handsome and of different forms; all of them accessible and abounding in trees of a thousand kinds, high, and appearing as if they would reach the skies. And I am assured that the latter never lose their fresh foliage, as far as I can understand, for I saw them as fresh and flourishing as those of Spain in the month of May. Some were in blossom, some bearing fruit, and others in other states, according to their nature.

"The nightingale and a thousand kinds of birds enliven the woods with their song, in the month of November, wherever I went. There are seven or eight kinds of palms, of various elegant forms, besides various other trees, fruits, and herbs. The pines of this island are magnificent. It has also extensive plains, honey, and a great variety of birds and fruits. It has many metal mines, and a population innumerable.

"Espanola is a wonderful island, with mountains, groves, plains, and the country generally beautiful and rich for planting and sowing, for rearing sheep and cattle of all kinds, and ready for towns and cities. The harbours must be seen to be appreciated; rivers are plentiful and large and of excellent water; the greater part of them contain gold. There is a great difference between the trees, fruits, and herbs of this island and those of Juana. In this island there are many spices, and large mines of gold and other metals.

"The people of this island and of all the others which I have discovered or heard of, both men and women, go naked as they were born, although some of the women wear leaves of herbs or a cotton covering made on purpose. They have no iron or steel, nor any weapons; not that they are not a well-disposed people and of fine stature, but they are timid to a degree. They have no other arms excepting spears made of cane, to which they fix at the end a sharp piece of wood, and then dare not use even these. Frequently I had occasion to send two or three of my men onshore to some settlement for information, where there would be multitudes of them; and as soon as they saw our people they would run away every soul, the father leaving his child; and this was not because any one had done them harm, for rather at every cape where I had landed and been able to communicate with them I have made them presents of cloth and many other things without receiving anything in return; but because they are so timid. Certainly, where they have confidence and forget their fears, they are so open-hearted and liberal with all they possess that it is scarcely to be believed without seeing it. If anything that they have is asked of them they never deny it; on the contrary, they will offer it. Their generosity is so great that they would give anything, whether it is costly or not, for anything of every kind that is offered them and be contented with it. I was obliged to prevent such worth less things being given them as pieces of broken basins, broken glass, and bits of shoe-latchets, although when they obtained them they esteemed them as if they had been the greatest of treasures. One of the seamen for a latchet received a piece of gold weighing two dollars and a half, and others, for other things of much less value, obtained more. Again, for new silver coin they would give everything they possessed, whether it was worth two or three doubloons or one or two balls of cotton. Even for pieces of broken pipe-tubes they would take them and give anything for them, until, when I thought it wrong, I prevented it. And I made them presents of thousands of things which I had, that I might win their esteem, and also that they might be made good Christians and be disposed to the service of Your Majesties and the whole Spanish nation, and help us to obtain the things which we require and of which there is abundance in their country.

"And these people appear to have neither religion nor idolatry, except that they believe that good and evil come from the skies; and they firmly believed that our ships and their crews, with myself, came from the skies, and with this persuasion,—after having lost their fears, they always received us. And yet this does not proceed from ignorance, for they are very ingenious, and some of them navigate their seas in a wonderful manner and give good account of things, but because they never saw people dressed or ships like ours.

"And as soon as I arrived in the Indies, at the first island at which I touched, I captured some of them, that we might learn from them and obtain intelligence of what there was in those parts. And as soon as we understood each other they were of great service to us; but yet, from frequent conversation which I had with them, they still believe we came from the skies. These were the first to express that idea, and others ran from house to house, and to the neighbouring villages, crying out, "Come and see the people from the skies." And thus all of them, men and women, after satisfying themselves of their safety, came to us without reserve, great and small, bringing us something to eat and drink, and which they gave to us most affectionately.

"They have many canoes in those islands propelled by oars, some of them large and others small, and many of them with eight or ten paddles of a side, not very wide, but all of one trunk, and a boat cannot keep way with them by oars, for they are incredibly fast; and with these they navigate all the islands, which are innumerable, and obtain their articles of traffic. I have seen some of these canoes with sixty or eighty men in them, and each with a paddle.

"Among the islands I did not find much diversity of formation in the people, nor in their customs, nor their language. They all understand each other, which is remarkable; and I trust Your Highnesses will determine on their being converted to our faith, for which they are very well disposed.

"I have already said that I went 107 leagues along the coast of Juana, from east to west. Thus, according to my track, it is larger than England and Scotland together, for, besides these 107 leagues, there were further west two provinces to which I did not go, one of which is called Cibau, the people of which are born with tails; which provinces must be about fifty or sixty leagues long, according to what I can make out from the Indians I have with me, who know all the islands. The other island (Espanola) is larger in circuit than the whole of Spain, from the Straits of Gibralter (the Columns) to Fuentarabia in Biscay, as I sailed 138 long leagues in a direct line from west to east. Once known it must be desired, and once seen one desires never to leave it; and which, being taken possession of for their Highnesses, and the people being at present in a condition lower than I can possibly describe, the Sovereigns of Castile may dispose of it in any manner they please in the most convenient places. In this Espanola, and in the best district, where are gold mines, and, on the other side, from thence to terra firma, as well as from thence to the Great Khan, where everything is on a splendid scale—I have taken possession of a large town, to which I gave the name of La Navidad, and have built a fort in it, in every respect complete. And I have left sufficient people in it to take care of it, with artillery and provisions for more than a year; also a boat and coxswain with the equipments, in complete friendship with the King of the islands, to that degree that he delighted to call me and look on me as his brother. And should they fall out with these people, neither he nor his subjects know anything of weapons, and go naked, as I have said, and they are the most timorous people in the world. The few people left there are sufficient to conquer the country, and the island would thus remain without danger to them, they keeping order among themselves.

"In all these islands it appeared to me the men are contented with one wife, but to their governor or king they allow twenty. The women seem to work more than the men. I have not been able to discover whether they respect personal property, for it appeared to me things were common to all, especially in the particular of provisions. Hitherto I have not seen in any of these islands any monsters, as there were supposed to be; the people, on the contrary, are generally well formed, nor are they black like those of the Guinea, saving their hair, and they do not reside in places exposed to the sun's rays. It is true that the sun is most powerful there, and it is only twenty-six degrees from the equator. In this last winter those islands which were mountainous were cold, but they were accustomed to it, with good food and plenty of spices and hot nutriment. Thus I have found no monsters nor heard of any, except at an island which is the second in going to the Indies, and which is inhabited by a people who are considered in all the islands as ferocious, and who devour human flesh. These people have many canoes, which scour all the islands of India, and plunder all they can. They are not worse formed than the others, but they wear the hair long like women, and use bows and arrows of the same kind of cane, pointed with a piece of hard wood instead of iron, of which they have none. They are fierce compared with the other people, who are in general but sad cowards; but I do not consider them in any other way superior to them. These are they who trade in women, who inhabit the first island met with in going from Spain to the Indies, in which there are no men whatever. They have no effeminate exercise, but bows and arrows, as before said, of cane, with which they arm themselves, and use shields of copper, of which they have plenty.

"There is another island, I am told, larger than Espanola, the natives of which have no hair. In this there is gold without limit, and of this and the others I have Indians with me to witness.

"In conclusion, referring only to what has been effected by this voyage, which was made with so much haste, Your Highnesses may see that I shall find as much gold as desired with the very little assistance afforded to me; there is as much spice and cotton as can be wished for, and also gum, which hitherto has only been found in Greece, in the island of Chios, and they may sell it as they please, and the mastich, as much as may be desired, and slaves, also, who will be idolators. And I believe that I have rhubarb, and cinnamon, and a thousand other things I shall find, which will be discovered by those whom I have left behind, for I did not stop at any cape when the wind enabled me to navigate, except at the town of Navidad, where I was very safe and well taken care of. And in truth much more I should have done if the ships had served me as might have been expected. This is certain, that the Eternal God our Lord gives all things to those who obey Him, and the victory when it seems impossible, and this, evidently, is an instance of it, for although people have talked of these lands, all was conjecture unless proved by seeing them, for the greater part listened and judged more by hearsay than by anything else.

"Since, then, our Redeemer has given this victory to our illustrious King and Queen and celebrated their reigns by such a great thing, all Christendom should rejoice and make great festivals, and give solemn thanks to the Blessed Trinity, with solemn praises for the exaltation of so much people to our holy faith; and next for the temporal blessings which not only Spain but they will enjoy in becoming Christians, and which last may shortly be accomplished.

"Written in the caravel off Santa Maria; on the eighteenth of
    February, ninety-three."

The following postscript was added to the letter before it was despatched:

"After writing the above, being in the Castilian Sea (off the coast of Castile), I experienced so severe a wind from south and south-east that I have been obliged to run to-day into this port of Lisbon, and only by a miracle got safely in, from whence I intended to write to Your Highnesses. In all parts of the Indies I have found the weather like that of May, where I went in ninety-three days, and returned in seventy-eight, saving these thirteen days of bad weather that I have been detained beating about in this sea. Every seaman here says that never was so severe a winter, nor such loss of ships."

On the Friday a messenger came from the King in the person of Don Martin de Noronha, a relative of Columbus by marriage, and one who had perhaps looked down upon him in the days when he attended the convent chapel at Lisbon, but who was now the bearer of a royal invitation and in the position of a mere envoy. Columbus repaired to Paraiso where the King was, and where he was received with great honour.

King John might well have been excused if he had felt some mortification at this glorious and successful termination of a project which had been offered to him and which he had rejected; but he evidently behaved with dignity and a good grace, and did everything that he could to help Columbus. It was extremely unlikely that he had anything to do with the insult offered to Columbus at the Azores, for though he was bitterly disappointed that the glory of this discovery belonged to Spain and not to Portugal, he was too much of a man to show it in this petty and revengeful manner. He offered to convey Columbus by land into Spain; but the Admiral, with a fine dramatic sense, preferred to arrive by sea on board of all that was left of the fleet with which he had sailed. He sailed for Seville on Wednesday, March 13th, but during the next day, when he was off Cape Saint Vincent, he evidently changed his mind and decided to make for Palos. Sunrise on Friday saw him off the bar of Saltes, with the white walls of La Rabida shining on the promontory among the dark fir-trees. During the hours in which he stood off and on waiting for the tide he was able to recognise again all the old landmarks and the scenes which had been so familiar to him in those busy days of preparation nine months before; and at midday he sailed in with the flood tide and dropped his anchor again in the mud of the river by Palos.

The caravel had been sighted some time before, probably when she was standing off, the bar waiting for the tide; she was flying the Admiral's flag and there was no mistaking her identity; and we can imagine the news spreading throughout the town of Palos, and reaching Huelva, and one by one the bells beginning to ring, and the places of business to be closed, and the people to come pouring out into the streets to be ready to greet their friends. Some more impatient than the others would sail out in fishing-boats to get the first news; and I should be surprised to know that a boat did not put off from the little pier beneath La Rabida, to row round the point and out to where the Nina was lying—to beyond the Manto Bank. When the flood began to make over the bar and to cover the long sandbank that stretches from the island of Saltes, the Nina came gliding in, greeted by every joyful sound and signal that the inhabitants of the two seaports could make. Every one hurried down to Palos as the caravel rounded the Convent Point. Hernando, Marchena, and good old Juan Perez were all there, we may be sure. Such excitements, such triumphs as the bronzed, white-bearded Admiral steps ashore at last, and is seized by dozens of eager hands! Such excitements as all the wives and inamoratas of the Rodrigos and Juans and Franciscos rush to meet the swarthy voyagers and cover them with embraces; such disappointments also, when it is realised that some two score of the company are still on a sunbaked island infinitely far over the western horizon.

Tears of joy and grief, shouts and feastings, firing of guns and flying of flags, processions and receptions with these the deathless day is filled; and the little Nina, her purpose staunchly fulfilled, swings deserted on the turning tide, the ripples of her native Tinto making a familiar music under her bowsprit.

And in the evening, with the last of the flood, another ship comes gliding round the point and up the estuary. The inhabitants of Palos have all left the shore and are absorbed in the business of welcoming the great man; and there is no one left to notice or welcome the Pinta. For it is she that, by a strange coincidence, and after many dangers and distresses endured since she had parted company from the Nina in the storm, now has made her native port on the very same day as the Nina. Our old friend Martin Alonso Pinzon is on board, all the fight and treachery gone out of him, and anxious only to get home unobserved. For (according to the story) he had made the port of Bayona on the north-west coast of Spain, and had written a letter from there to the Sovereigns announcing his arrival and the discoveries that he had made; and it is said that he had received an unpleasant letter in return, reproaching him for not waiting for his commander and forbidding him to come to Court. This story is possible if his letter reached the Sovereigns after the letter from the Admiral; for it is probable that Columbus may have reported some of Martin's doings to them.

Be that as it may, there are no flags and guns for him as he comes creeping in up the river; his one anxiety is to avoid the Admiral and to get home as quickly and quietly as he can. For he is ill, poor Martin Alonso; whether from a broken heart, as the early historians say, or from pure chagrin and disappointment, or, as is more likely, from some illness contracted on the voyage, it is impossible to say. He has endured his troubles and hardships like all the rest of them; no less skilfully than Columbus has he won through that terrible tempest of February; and his foolish and dishonest conduct has deprived him not only of the rewards that he tried to steal, but of those which would otherwise have been his by right. He creeps quietly ashore and to his home, where at any rate we may hope that there is some welcome for him; takes to his bed, turns his face to the wall; and dies in a few days. So farewell to Martin Alonso, who has borne us company thus far. He did not fail in the great matters of pluck and endurance and nautical judgment, but only in the small matters of honesty and decent manly conduct. We will not weep for Martin Alonso; we will make our farewells in silence, and leave his deathbed undisturbed by any more accusations or reproaches.

The End